Accents

any design in a tag - real string

Use this section when you're struggling to find the perfect accent for your page. Don't hesitate to change shapes, combine ideas, or substitute stickers, punches or handmade elements for the ones sketched here!

See page 32 for supplies.

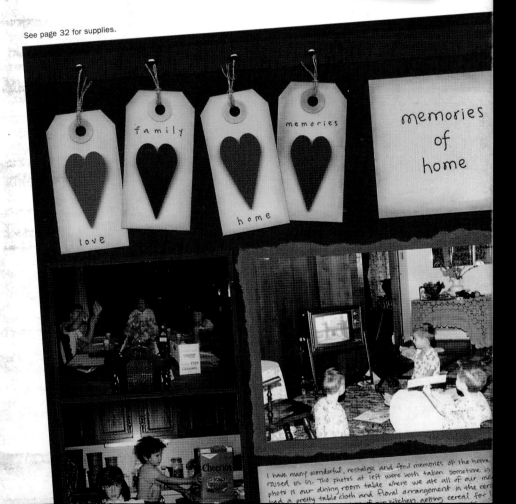

family

memories

home

love

memories of home

I have many wonderful, nostalgic and fond memories of the home I was raised us in. The photos at left were both taken sometime in [...] photo is our dining room table where we ate all of our m[...] had a pretty table cloth and floral arrangement in the cen[...] kitchen getting cereal for [...]

double
layers of
torn

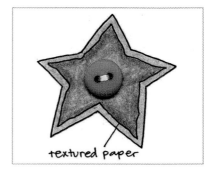

textured paper

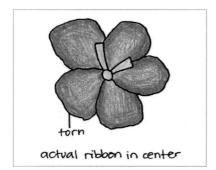

torn

actual ribbon in center

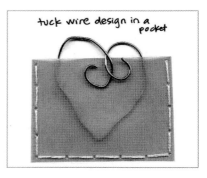

tuck wire design in a pocket

any design
in a tag
real string

actual vellum
& grommet

stitch
part of
a design

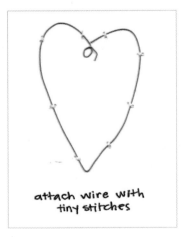

attach wire with
tiny stitches

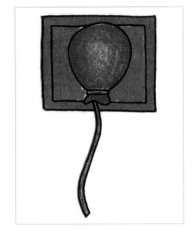

anything hanging
from hanger

tall
cake

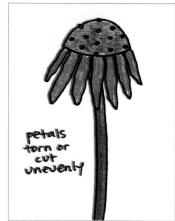

petals
torn or
cut
unevenly

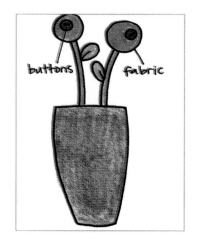

buttons   fabric

actual
string

folded strips of
cardstock

vellum flowers on vellum blocks; attach with brads

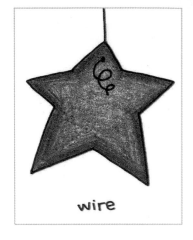

wire

swirly shapes with twine, string or wire

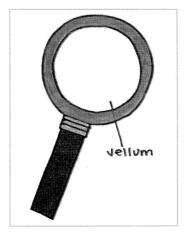

vellum

vellum over punch

vellum behind

use actual string/ribbon

smaller circles in larger ones

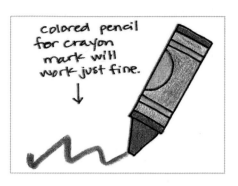

colored pencil for crayon mark will work just fine.

ribbon or twine

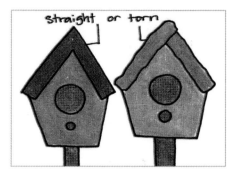

straight or torn

any accents in a vellum pocket

hang punch from a template letter

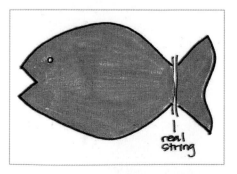

real string

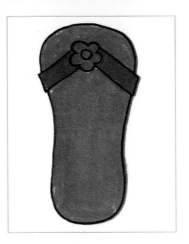

torn or texture

bubbles with light
blue cardstock and
chalked around edges

primitive heart punch

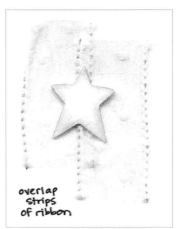

overlap
strips
of ribbon

strip of
cardstock at
the top of
accent
blocks to
look like
clothespins

plastic
gems

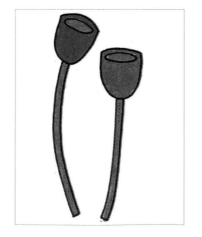

eyelet in the center

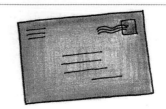

envelope
(fun idea for new
home pages, etc.)

torn edges

little knot at the top

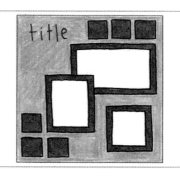

title

any
state

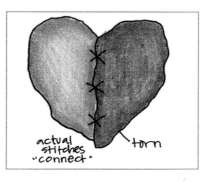

actual
stitches
"connect"

torn

vellum
punches

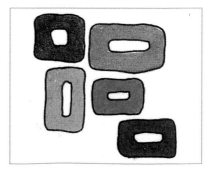

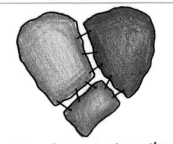

torn & stitched together

stitch border around
an accent

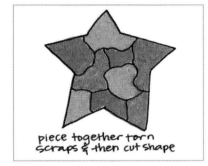

piece together torn
scraps & then cut shape

Simple
punch
in
simple
torn
block

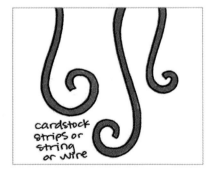

cardstock
strips or
string
or wire

houses

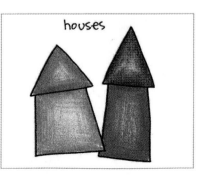

cut out
design
with a
craft knife

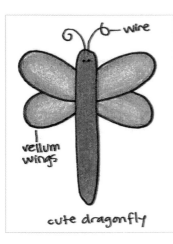

wire

vellum
wings

cute dragonfly

grommets as
flower centers

with or without ornaments

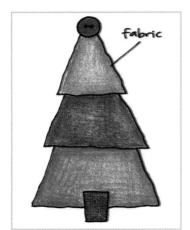

fabric

mulberry paper behind

string or wire

velvet paper stitched onto the paper

hang stockings from actual string

accents
on felt

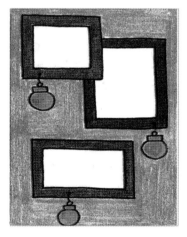

tag

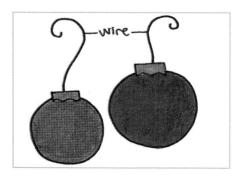

wire

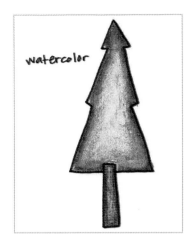

watercolor

chalk around
for glow effect

real
button

actual
stitches
or with
a pen

string or ribbon

tip: use circle punch and metallic paper

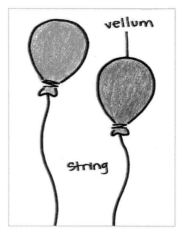

vellum

String

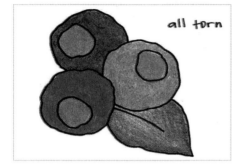

all torn

dangle GROUPS of accents and tie a knot at top

sheer/ netting over accent

flames can be made of vellum

string and rings

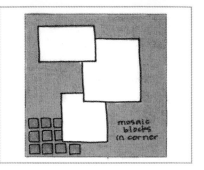

mosaic blocks in corner

torn edges

scene on journal block

hand-cut swirl

Flames

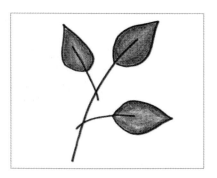

rocks with optional grass (green cardstock strips)

simple leaves

leaves are separate...

oval posies

...or touching

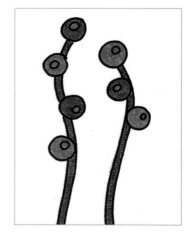

plastic gems as flower centers

laminate flowers, leaves, punches, etc. (with the Xyron), cut box shape around & mount on pop dots

brads on blocks &
blocks lifted on pop dots

torn layers
&chalked edges

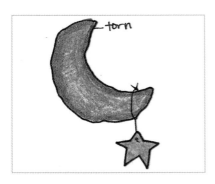

— thin strips
of green
cardstock

— punches

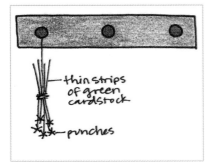

— torn

dangle
anything
from top
of page

any
flag

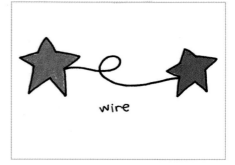

wire

in various places on layout

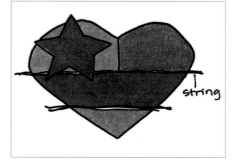

string

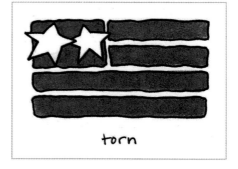

torn

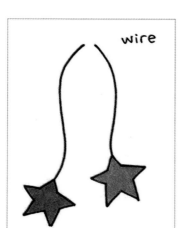

wire

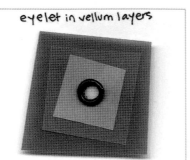
eyelet in vellum layers

fabric & button

delicate snowflake

heart tucked in a little envelope

twine around cardstock

dangle any two
accents from brad

contemporary-
style gift

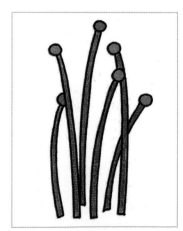

geometric collage with vellum

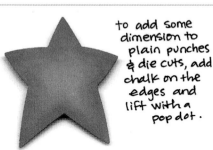

to add some dimension to plain punches & die cuts, add chalk on the edges and lift with a pop dot.

simple designs stitched

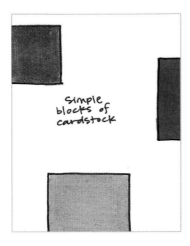

simple blocks of cardstock

vellum blocks over punches

accent designs with beads (stitch them on with thread)

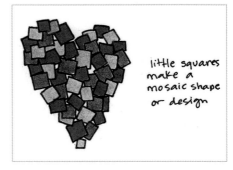

little squares make a mosaic shape or design

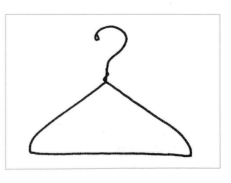

real
pressed
flowers

actual
tissue
paper

just
buttons

simple fabric blocks
(optional: include an
eyelet in the center)

block smaller
than accent

for accents or letters

any
embossed
design

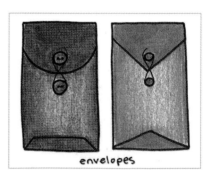

envelopes

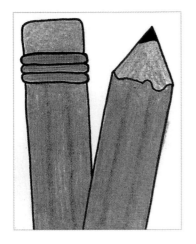

wire or
string "holds"
accent down

brick

an "actual" scroll,
rolled & tied

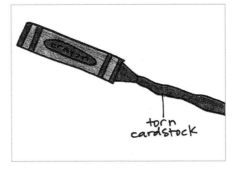

torn
cardstock

torn & folded

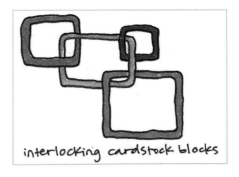

interlocking cardstock blocks

push pin

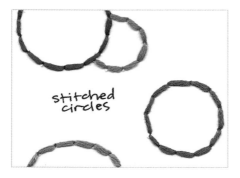

title — string

— punches

stitched
circles

rings

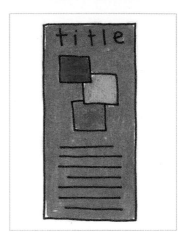

title

form leaf with
string or wire

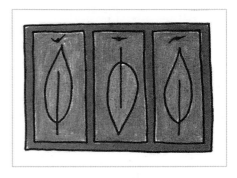

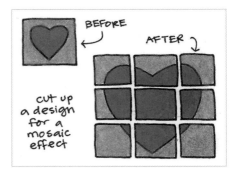

BEFORE

AFTER

cut up a design for a mosaic effect

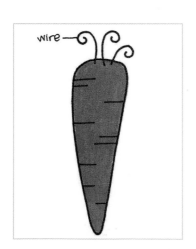

wire

wire "swirly" at the top of any design, journal block or whatever!

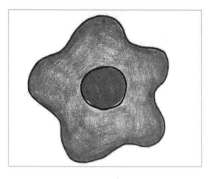

brush
pen
strokes

Mickey made of buttons
(stitched on)

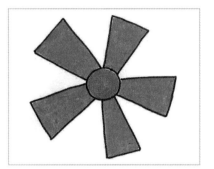

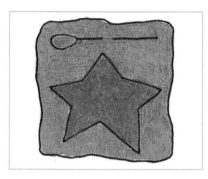

hula skirt
made of raffia

fabric
buttons

creative
string

sheer fabric

torn strips

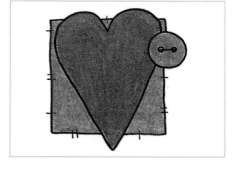

watercolor

First, cut out
shape from
white cardstock
and then
watercolor
(2 colors
shown here)
and mount!

Great for Easter

"My Cousins"

SUPPLIES

Vellum: Paper Adventures
Craft wire: Darice
Pen: American Crafts
Colored pencil:
Prismacolor, Sanford
MCC inspiration: Becky created
the leaf accent using the
sketches on pages 4 and 26.

"Fourth of July"

SUPPLIES

Star punch: Emagination Crafts
Pen: Zig Writer, EK Success
Other: Fabric
MCC inspiration: Becky created
the flag accent using the sketch
on page 19.

PHOTOS BY ANITA MATEJKA

"Roca Berry Farm"

SUPPLIES
Leaf punch:
Emagination Crafts
Pen: Zig Millennium,
EK Success
Colored pencils:
Prismacolor, Sanford
Pop dots:
Mrs. Grossman's
Other: Becky used
a Xyron machine
to laminate the
leaf accents.
MCC inspiration:
Becky created
the leaf accents
using the sketch
on page 17.

"Finding Our Home"

SUPPLIES
Patterned paper:
Making Memories
Pens: Zig Writer,
EK Success
MCC inspiration:
Becky created the
house accents using
the sketch on page 9.

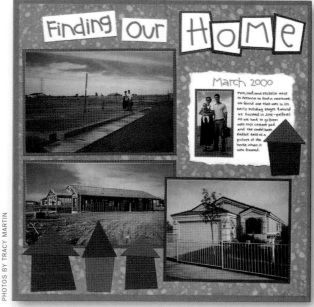

PHOTOS BY TRACY MARTIN

"Kevin's High School Graduation"

SUPPLIES
Pen: Pigma Micron, Sakura
Grommet: Impress Rubber Stamps
Silver rope: Needloft
Colored pencil: Prismacolor, Sanford
Pop dots: Hampton Arts
Other: Red twine
MCC inspiration: Becky created the tag accent using the sketches on pages 1 and 25.

"Memories of Home"

SUPPLIES
Heart punch: Emagination Crafts
Tags: DMD Industries
Chalk: Craf-T Products
Brads: American Pin and Fastener
Pen: Pigma Micron, Sakura
Other: Twine
MCC inspiration: Becky created the heart accents using the sketch on page 27.

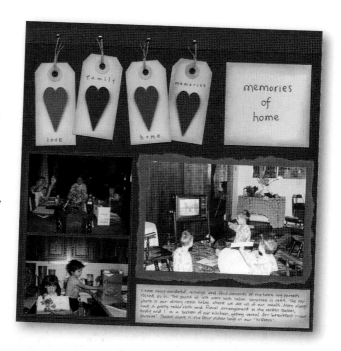

Borders

$\mathcal{U}$se these innovative borders to brighten any scrapbook page.

They're great as is, or use them to give you ideas for new borders to try!

See page 64 for supplies.

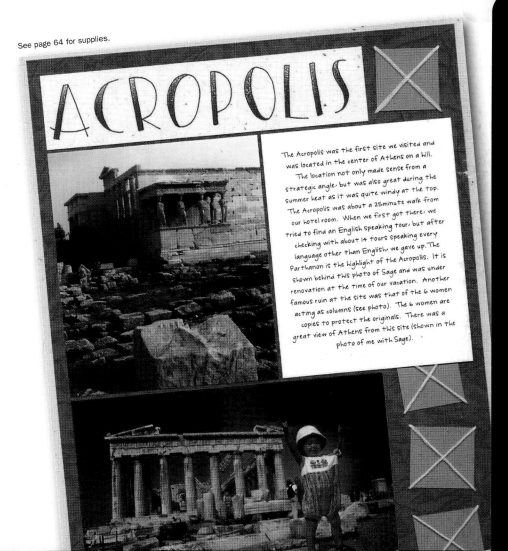

The Acropolis was the first site we visited and was located in the center of Athens on a hill.

The location not only made sense from a strategic angle, but was also great during the summer heat as it was quite windy at the top. The Acropolis was about a 25minute walk from our hotel room. When we first got there, we tried to find an English speaking tour, but after checking with about 14 tours speaking every language other than English we gave up. The Parthanon is the highlight of the Acropolis. It is shown behind this photo of Sage and was under renovation at the time of our vacation. Another famous ruin at the site was that of the 6 women acting as columns (see photo). The 6 women are copies to protect the originals. There was a great view of Athens from this site (shown in the photo of me with Sage).

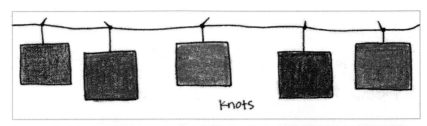

Knots

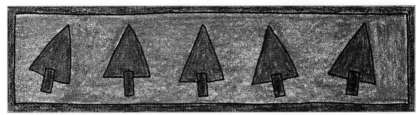

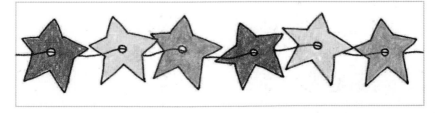

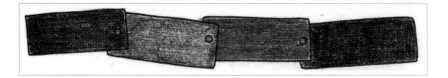

words on designer strip

simple strand of string/yarn

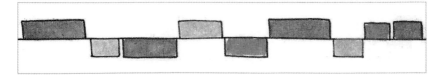

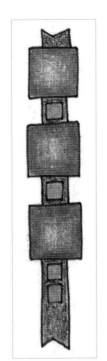

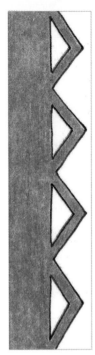

double brush strokes

gems

use real string / thread

simple torn strip

chalked

dirt (torn, chalked)

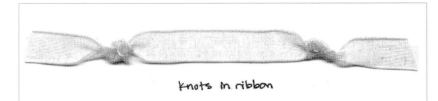

knots in ribbon

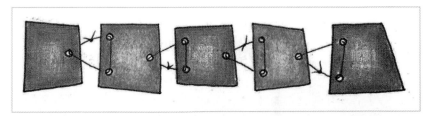

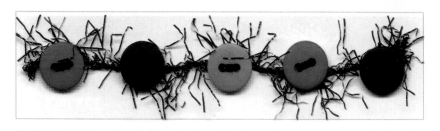

matted strips

brush strokes

snow (torn, chalked)

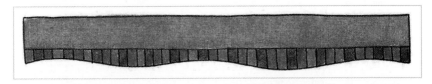

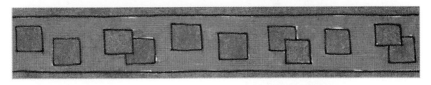

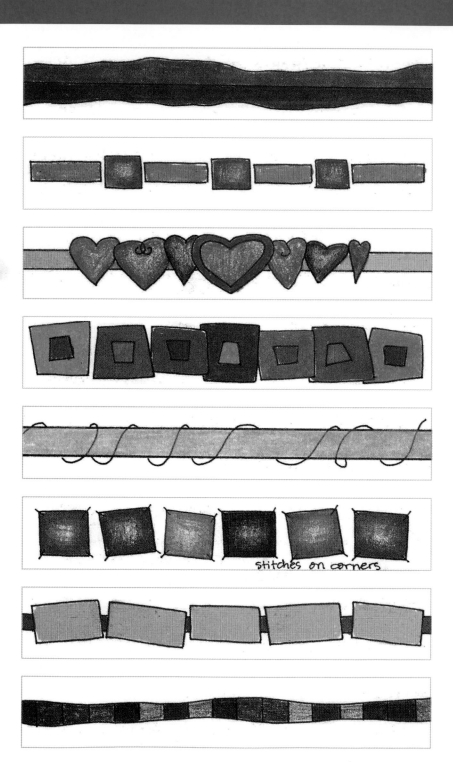

stitches on corners

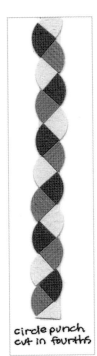

circle punch
cut in fourths

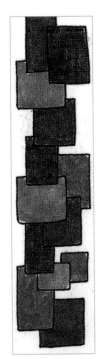

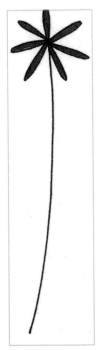

simple boxes

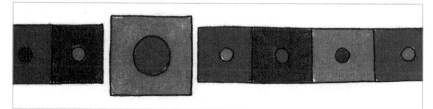

pen stitching around boxes

raffia

just a strip
of fabric

vellum
over torn
strip

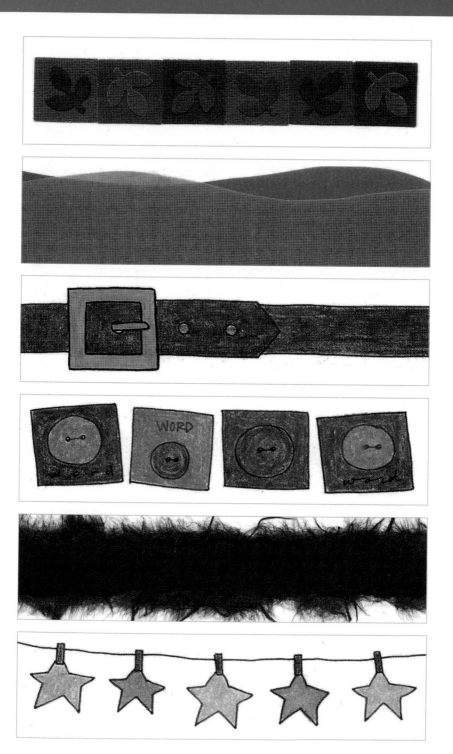

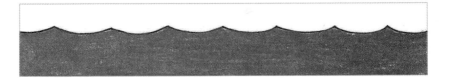

words words words words words word
s words words words words words w
rds words word words words words

little boxes
(square punch)
cut into
halves and
adhered,
touching

braid ANYthing! (this is raffia)

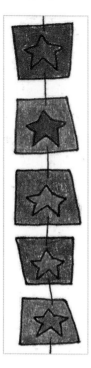

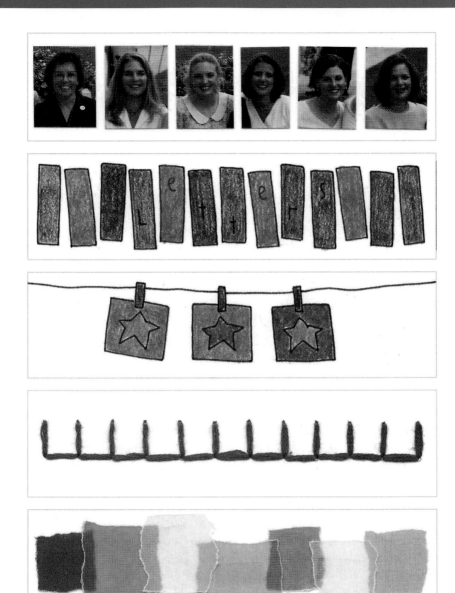

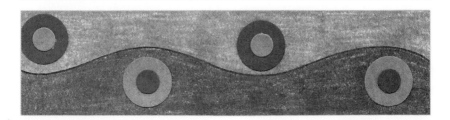

torn strips
to look
like grass

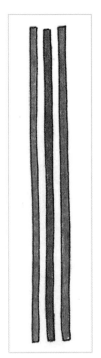

any
letter
or
shape

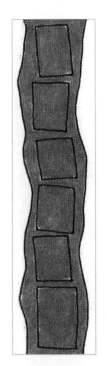

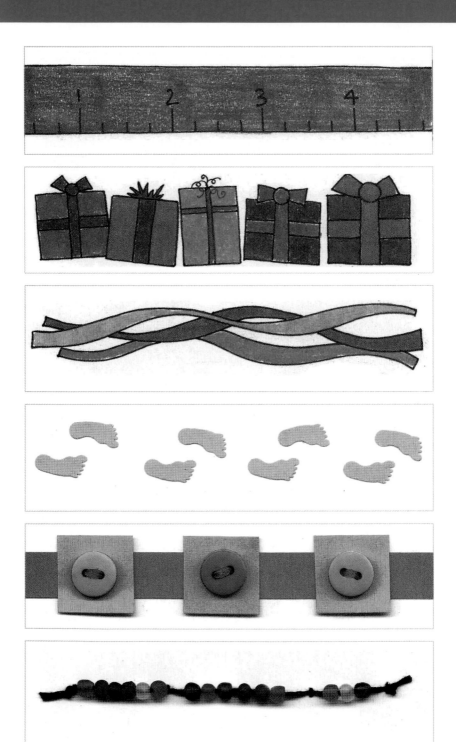

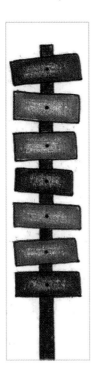

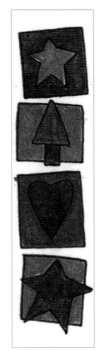

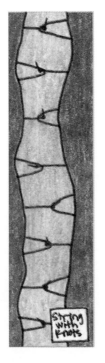

simple
strip of
pattern paper

string
with
knots

word

word

WORD

word

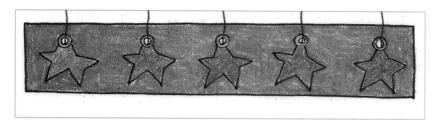

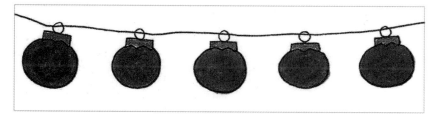

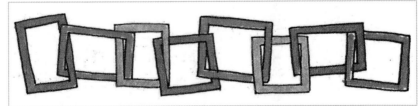

textures

wrinkled tissue paper

plain strip of cardstock with chalked edges

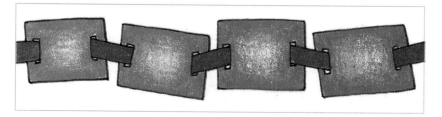

accents on vellum, over strip

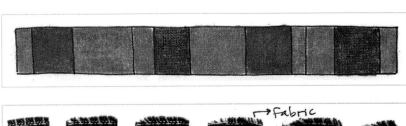

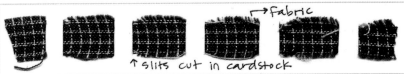

fabric

↑ slits cut in cardstock

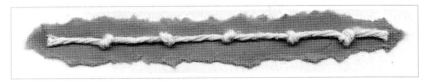

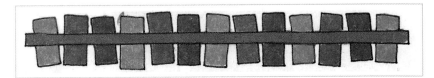

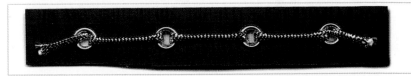

try string, too

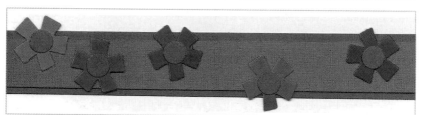

strips of raffia

books

crumpled vellum

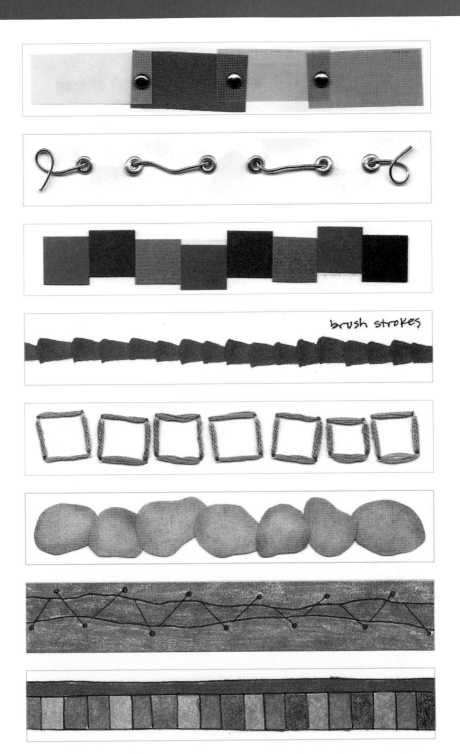

brush strokes

loop together string, wire, etc.

use thread for stitches

Knot in ribbon / fabric

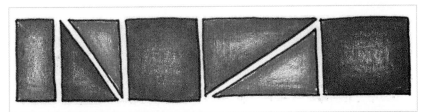

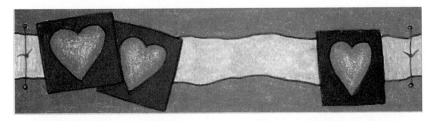

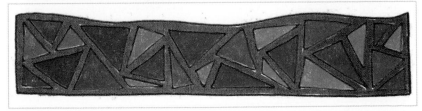

vellum stitched on top

(2 knots)

yarn

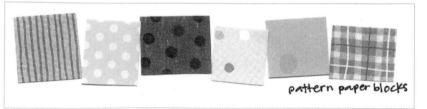

pattern paper blocks

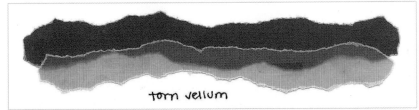

torn vellum

It was a real treat to have a girls-only day at Disneyland! Olivia thoroughly enjoyed being spoiled by her grandma and aunts.

"Mickey Ears"

SUPPLIES
Circle punches: Family Treasures (large), McGill (small)
Pen: Pigma Micron, Sakura
MCC inspiration: Becky created the hanging border for her page using the sketch on page 44.

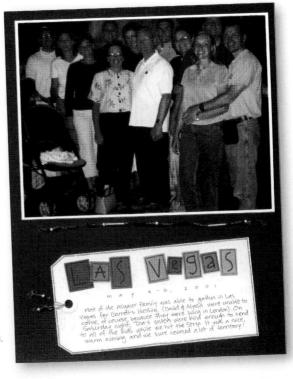

"Las Vegas"

SUPPLIES
Tag accent: DMD Industries
Craft wire: Artistic Wire
Beads: Westrim
Pen: Pigma Micron, Sakura
MCC inspiration: Becky created the bead border using the sketch on page 53.

Las Vegas

m a y   4 - 6,   2 0 0 1

Most of the Allgaier family was able to gather in Las Vegas for Garrett's blessing. (David & Alyssa were unable to come, of course, because they were living in London.) On Saturday night, Tim's sisters were kind enough to tend to all of the kids while we hit the Strip. It was a nice, warm evening and we sure covered a lot of territory!

PHOTOS BY DAWN DELLASTATIOUS

"Clown Party"

SUPPLIES
Patterned paper:
Paperfever
Lettering template:
Frances Meyer
MCC inspiration:
Becky created the
picture border for
her page using the
sketch on page 47.

"Abiqua Falls"

SUPPLIES
Chalk: Stampin' Up!
Pen: Zig Writer,
EK Success
MCC inspiration: Becky
created the shadowed
border using the sketch
on page 54.

PHOTOS BY DANIEL HIGGINS

"ACROPOLIS"

The Acropolis was the first site we visited and was located in the center of Athens on a hill. The location not only made sense from a strategic angle, but was also great during the summer heat as it was quite windy at the top. The Acropolis was about a 25minute walk from our hotel room. When we first got there, we tried to find an English speaking tour, but after checking with about 15 tours speaking every language other than English we gave up. The Parthenon is the highlight of the Acropolis. It is shown behind this photo of Sage and was under renovation at the time of our vacation. Another famous ruin at the site was that of the 6 women acting as columns (see photo). The 6 women are copies to protect the originals. There was a great view of Athens from this site (shown in the photo of me with Sage).

"Acropolis"

SUPPLIES
Computer font: CK Jot, "The Art of Creative Lettering" CD, *Creating Keepsakes*
Colored pencils: Prismacolor, Sanford
Pen: Pigma Micron, Sakura
Embroidery floss: DMC
MCC inspiration: Becky created the block border using the sketch on page 35.

Water-Skiing!

Lake Pleasant July 13-14

Bill called us on Friday afternoon & invited us to go water-skiing with him (& his sister, Julie, and a friend from work). We had so much fun that we went again early Saturday morning!

"Water-Skiing"

SUPPLIES
Colored pencils: Prismacolor, Sanford
Pen: Pigma Micron, Sakura
MCC inspiration: Becky created the striped border using the sketch on page 40.

Journaling & Titles

Use this section to create and place your journaling and titles in new ways. Feel free to experiment with lettering templates, computer fonts, alphabet stickers and your own handwriting when you use these ideas!

journaling on mat

Title

See page 96 for supplies.

October 2000

We (Morgan, Mychaela and Mom) went to visit a pumpkin patch with a friend, Michael Kariker. Our destination was In the Pines, Hindsville, Arkansas and it was just beautiful!

PUMPKIN

shade
outside
to
inside
(with pencils)

mix & match
edges

box outline only

journaling on mat

Designs on top

SUB TITLE

Title
blend two colors of colored pencils

JOURNALING and more journaling

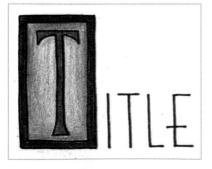
TITLE

Title
mix & match straight, crooked, ripped, matted...

slightly different letters
and an <u>occasional</u> box

vellum letters
overlap

all letter blocks
are torn

all blocks kept straight,
various heights

small block on title block

the date

template letters
in boxes
mixed with some
"plain" letters,
drawn.

...a "shapely" title

WAVY TITLES

draw freeform lines
(top & bottom),
write words and
then erase

hang letter boxes
from top of page

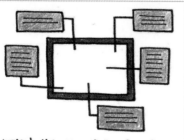

point things out in the photo

mat just one letter

"ground"-like border
at bottom of mat

accents on side of photo mat

each block is a
different color
(ex–cut from cardstock)

subtitle block behind/
beneath title

various blocks and
boxes

some letters in a
box, some not

shade in from top
and bottom with
colored pencils

accent letters
with punches

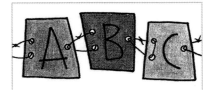

or make blocks larger
& include journaling
in each one

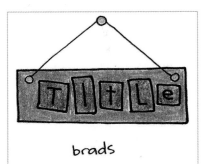

brads

draw outlines with pen,
shade with pencils,
alternating colors

draw a "slicing" line
through the word
and color two-tone

OFF—centered A N D RANDOM w o r d s

title blocks on photo

template letter
& then the rest of
the letters in boxes

one letter hangs
from top of page

dangle accent
from
template
letter

one letter in a block

trace letters with a
template & write
word through

strips of cardstock

title and journaling take up bottom 1/3

TITLE

title on matted strip across bottom

TITLE

TITLE

letter blocks on a strip

SUB title

trapezoid title flush @ top

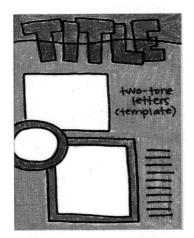

TITLE

two-tone letters (template)

title

title on a torn strip at the top of page

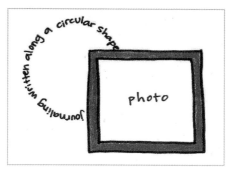

journaling written along a circular shape

photo

photo

S U B

Title

ripped block comes
off side of page

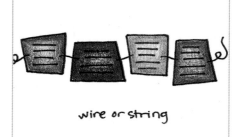

wire or string

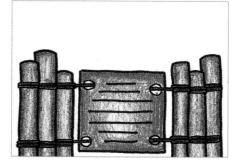

TITLE

torn bottom

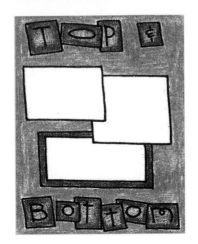

title strip is a wavy edge

pen stitch or actual thread

overlap letters on a strip

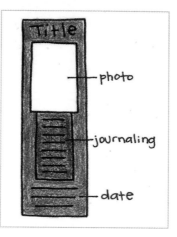

photo

journaling

date

journaling goes here

(along torn strip)

title

strip of paper
divides title and
journaling

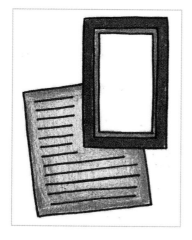

accents
in
boxes

journal block
has torn edges

vertical
title
with
date

vellum blocks behind
template letters

use craft knife to cut out
middles & put color behind

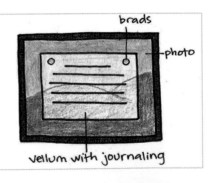

brads

photo

vellum with journaling

TITLE and an arched subtitle

brush strokes over box outlines.

vellum attached with brads

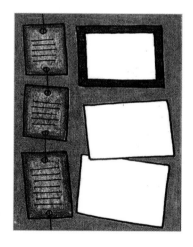

go DOWN the page

emphasize first letter (or initial)

accent
at the top
of the
journaling
block

Title

on vellum with
accents behind

creative string behind

string or wire

TITLE

chalk edges
of template letters
(cardstock)

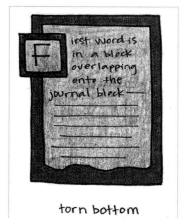

irst word is
in a block
overlapping
onto the
journal block

torn bottom

TITLE

TITLE

letters overlap
onto journal
block

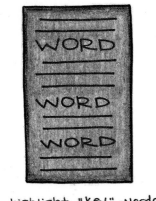

highlight "key" words

this is
a great
way to
include a LOT of journaling.

block with torn edge
at bottom

write journaling on a free-form line

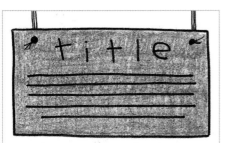

knots on top of holes

torn halves

vellum over designs

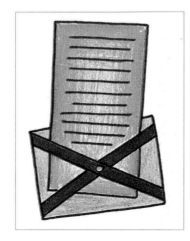

ribbon behind vellum

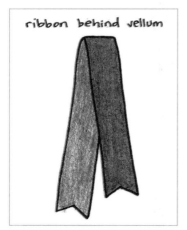

stitch with needle & thread

tied together

write title with

string

use
string
or
ribbon
or
twine
or
raffia

s u b t i t l e

square middles

connecting
letter blocks

hand-cut your
own letters

use real string

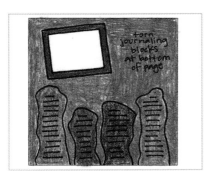

free-form cardstock strip

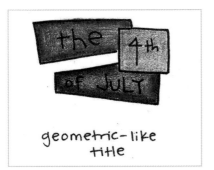

geometric-like title

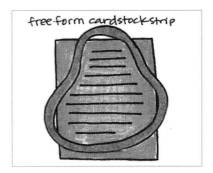

all in strips

use real string

journaling to accompany photo

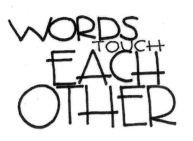

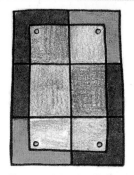

vellum attached to journal block with brads journaling on top

funky shape

subtitle

for the subtitle

top folded over & brads attach

brads & string

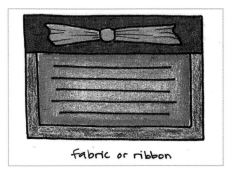

fabric or ribbon

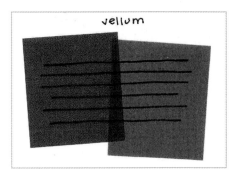

vellum

pen outline & color in.

first letter of journaling

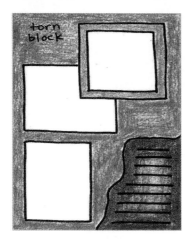

torn
block

TITLE HERE

try vellum strips

BLOCK
BEHIND
a
LONGER
TITLE

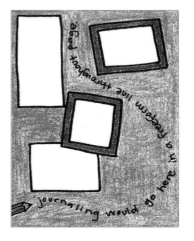

front page

journaling would go here in a freeform line

Hey

template
letters on
torn
strip

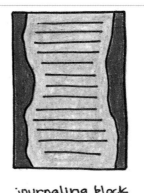

journaling block
edges torn on
the sides

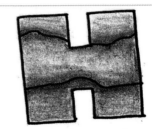

template letters
with torn layers

using a
brush pen

crookedly cut strips
of cardstock

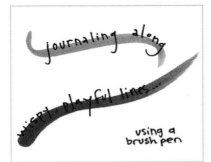

letters at bottoms of strips

or use cardstock
or pattern paper

trapezoid shapes with
torn top edges, all
placed on a
straight strip

title could be vellum
so you can see through

String wraps around letters

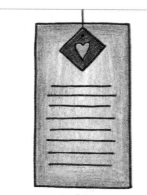

accent dangling
onto journal block

letter blocks
stitched together

shape behind one letter

with pattern paper

torn edge
can be dirt or
snow or grass

journaling written along torn edge

chalk over pen letters

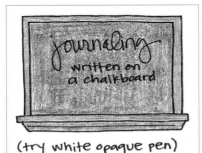

journaling
written on
a chalkboard

(try white opaque pen)

place these
at the bottom
of a page

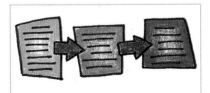

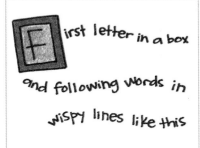

irst letter in a box
and following words in
wispy lines like this

helping the flow
of journaling

each letter is in a

string hangs from brads
or just draw lines

title

part of
word is
on the
journal
block

swirly outlining

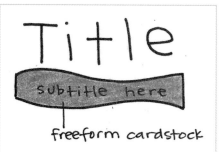

freeform cardstock

blocks in a wave

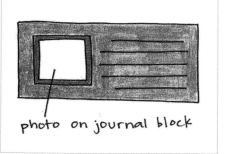

photo on journal block

plain hole or eyelet

cardstock box
outline around
template letters

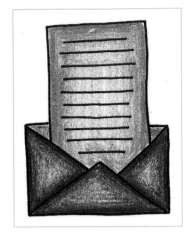

letters look like they're
hanging from
a clothesline

vellum mats

letters on torn
strip which is
on a journal block

overlaps onto half of title

(Idea: water photos)

title or journaling
written on vellum
with a cardstock
border
& shapes
behind

Strip of brown
cardstock to look
like a twig
(chalk edges)

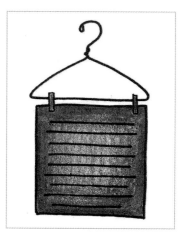

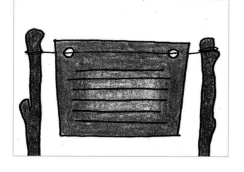

connect blocks
with ribbon
(and hole punch)

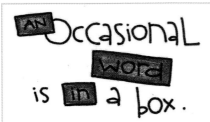

for titles or journaling

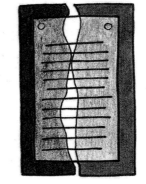

two parts of cardstock
behind vellum

layers of torn
letter blocks

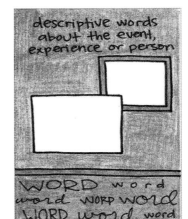

fabric or paper
strip under title

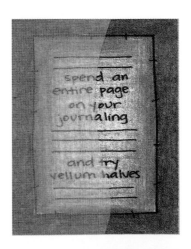

S   P   R   E   A   D

out

YOUR LETTERS

for an "airy" feel

We knew we wanted to do some sort of boating on our honeymoon. If we were to go sailing, we'd have to take a class so we decided to kayak instead. The water was freezing & there lots of sealions swimming around.

"Honeymoon Kayaking"

SUPPLIES

Pens: Zig Writer and Zig Scroll & Brush, EK Success
Colored pencils: Prismacolor, Sanford
MCC inspiration: Becky created the title and journaling using the sketches on pages 87 and 93.

"Swamp Safari Nature Walk"

SUPPLIES

Vellum: Paper Adventures
Computer font: CK Jot, "The Art of Creative Lettering" CD,
Creating Keepsakes
Brads: American Pin and Fastener
MCC inspiration: Becky created the journaling block using the sketch on page 75.

Emily's third Birthday

It's a tradition in our family that all the girls get an ice cream cake on their birthday. During a time of transition (our move to CA), it was nice to have tradition.

For Emily's 3rd birthday, we celebrated on the beach in Del Mar, CA with a theme of (what else?) Blues Clues!

We invited her grandma and aunt, Ashley, Kyle, and some friends from church... the perfect crowd.

Besides getting her very first bicycle, Emily had a very "Barbie Invasion" this year (and other fun things).

AUGUST 22, 2000

PHOTOS BY NANCI JARMAN

"Emily's Third Birthday"

SUPPLIES
Craft wire: Artistic Wire
Colored pencils: Prismacolor, Sanford
Pen: Zig Writer, EK Success
MCC inspiration: Becky created the journaling design using the sketch on page 72.

"Halloween"

SUPPLIES
Patterned paper: Creative Press
Computer font: CK Print, "The Best of Creative Lettering" CD Vol. 1, *Creating Keepsakes*
MCC inspiration: Becky created the title using the sketch on page 82.

HALLOWEEN

2000

PHOTO BY WENDY WOODBY

We met the Young family at CiCi's Pizza for dinner. Then on to the haunted house where the speaker kept saying "Bring me the girl with the tall hair". After being scared out of our skin we went trick-or-treating...of course!

"Pumpkin Patch"

SUPPLIES
Pumpkin die cuts:
My Mind's Eye
Pumpkin stickers:
DMD Industries
Grass punch:
EK Success
Computer fonts:
DJ Crayon, Fontastic! 1,
D.J. Inkers; CK Cursive,
"The Best of Creative
Lettering" CD Vol. 2,
Creating Keepsakes
Pop dots: Glue Dots
International
Pen: Zig Writer,
EK Success
Other: Twine
MCC inspiration: Becky
created the journaling
block and title using the
sketches on pages 66
and 92.

"PCO Graduate"

SUPPLIES
Patterned paper:
Colors By Design
Lettering template:
The C-Thru Ruler Co.
String: On the Surface
Pens: The Ultimate
Gel Pen (gold),
American Crafts;
Zig Writer, EK Success
MCC inspiration: Becky
created the journaling
block, title and subtitle
using the sketches on
pages 82 and 90.

Layout Design

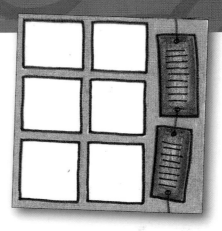

$\mathcal{A}$re all your layouts starting to look the same to you? Add some variety to your albums with these all-occasion layout designs.

See page 128 for supplies.

KAYLA'S
FiRST
BiRthdAY

SEPTEMBER
2000

Katelyn and Grant
cousin, Kayla, ha
her first birthda
party at her oth
grandparents' hor
She had great fu
with her cake (ca
you tell!?) and
even shared som
with her dad
(Cory).

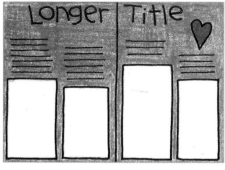

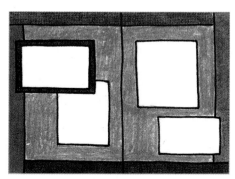

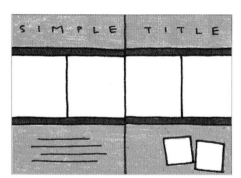

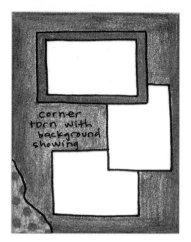

corner
torn with
background
showing

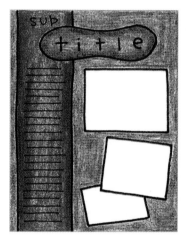

sub
title

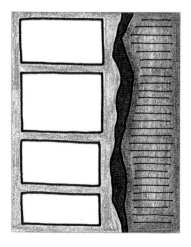

small photos ↓

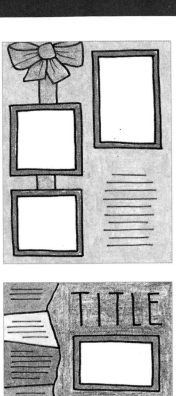

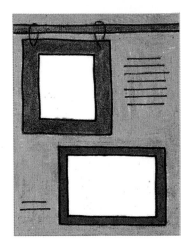

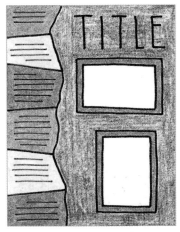

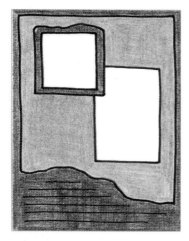

Title

across two-page spread

Panoramic Photo

Title

Title at top

title.

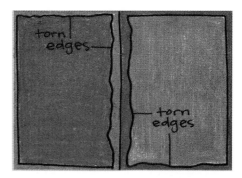

torn edges

torn edges

way to use
8½" x 11" paper
on 12" x 12" page

title

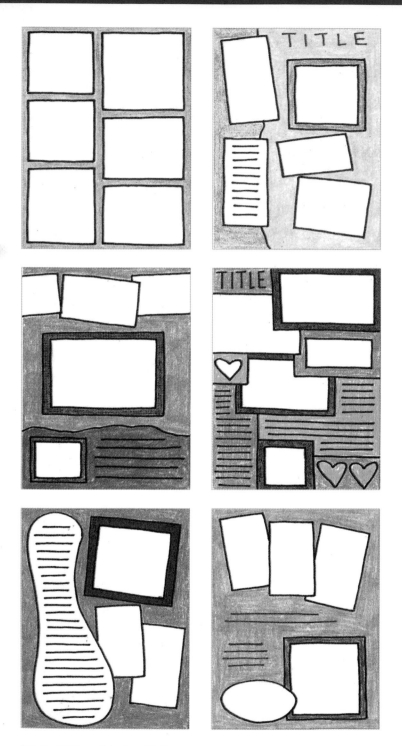

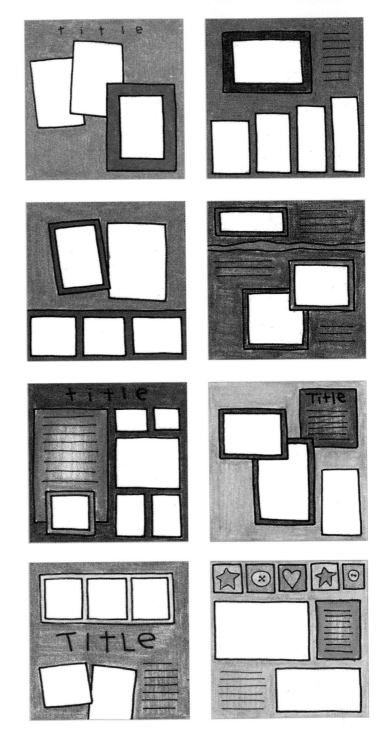

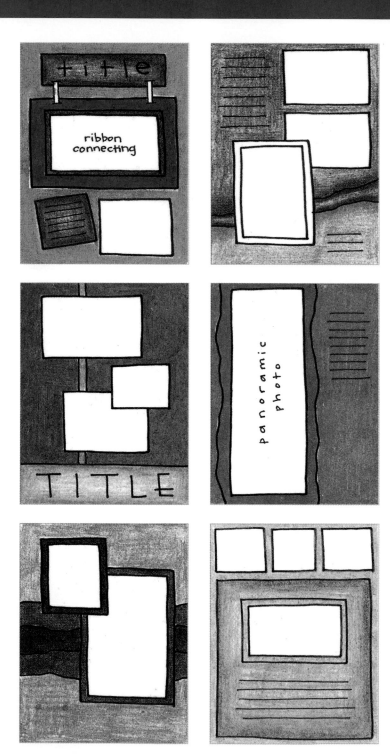

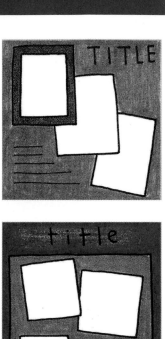

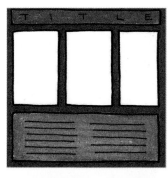

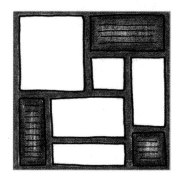

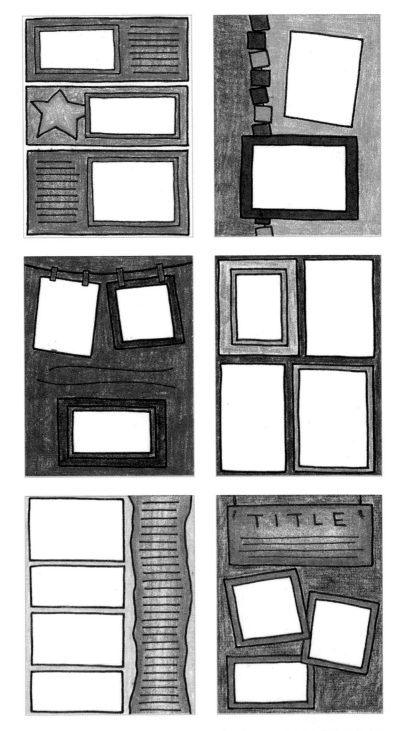

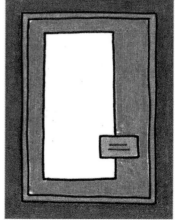

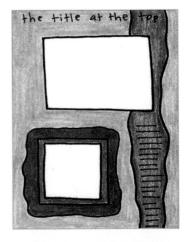

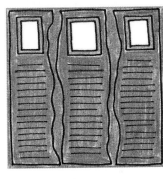

all are
photos,
touching

Title

TITLE

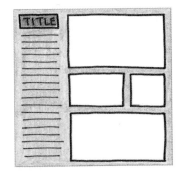

collaged photos touch

TITLE

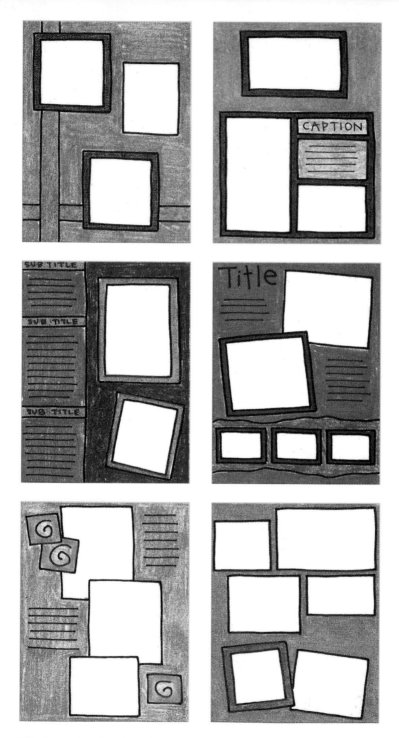

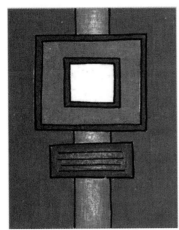

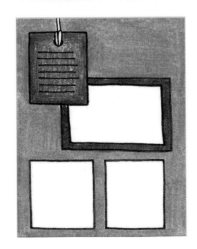

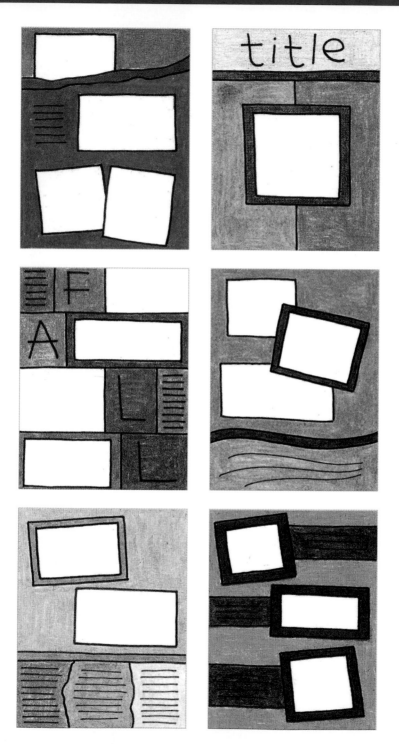

title

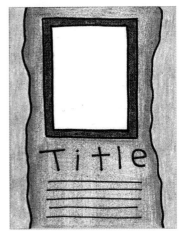

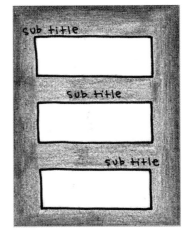

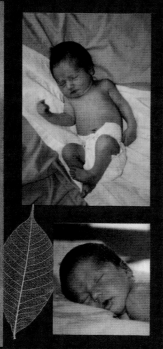

"Dear Matthew"

SUPPLIES

Patterned paper: Carolee's Creations
Leaf accent: Black Ink
Computer font: CK Simple, "The Art of Creative Lettering" CD, *Creating Keepsakes*
MCC inspiration: Becky got the layout placement idea from the sketch on page 109.

Halloween Train Ride 2000

"Halloween Train Ride 2000"

SUPPLIES

Computer font: DJ Fancy, Fontastic! 1, D.J. Inkers
MCC inspiration: Becky got the layout placement idea from the sketch on page 112.

"Our Family Line"

SUPPLIES

Pen: Zig Writer, EK Success
Chalk: Craf-T Products
String: On the Surface
Brad: American Pin and Fastener
MCC inspiration: Becky got the layout placement idea from the sketch on page 120.

My brother Steven (who is 4½ years older than me) and I have always been close. We share many interests and characteristics in common. One of those shared interests is our love for personal and family history.

We both have done our part to pull together the family newsletter (I was the "editor" as a child and Steven carries on that role today). When we were both living in Provo, we used to have "family history parties" (just the two of us), where we would exchange information and photos.

For Christmas, Steven drew my name in the family gift exchange. It was most appropriate that he made me this to hang in our home. The plaque reads "Our Family Line" and includes four generations of David's and my family names. It is 3D (in a shadow box) and has each name on a piece of clothing that hangs from clotheslines. It truly could NOT be any cuter. I love Steven!

"Ensenada, Mexico"

SUPPLIES

Pen: Zig Millennium, EK Success
MCC inspiration: Becky got the layout placement idea from the sketch on page 121.

PHOTOS BY STEPHANIE RAQUEL

"Fourth-Year Hike"

SUPPLIES
Vellum: Paper Adventures
Computer font: CK Sketch, "The Art of Creative Lettering" CD, *Creating Keepsakes*
Pen: The Ultimate Gel Pen, American Crafts
MCC inspiration: Becky got the layout placement idea from the sketch on page 99.

PHOTOS BY RACHAEL STONE

"Kayla's First Birthday"

SUPPLIES
Patterned paper: Paperfever
Pens: Zig Writer and Zig Scroll & Brush, EK Success
Pop dots: Close To My Heart
Other: Yarn
MCC inspiration: Becky got the layout placement idea from the sketch on page 97.

PHOTOS BY ANITA MATEJKA

Photo Mats

€mphasize your favorite photographs with creative photo mats using the sketches in this section. Remember how versatile the sketches are. You can easily change a leaf to a flower, for example, to change the whole look!

See page 159 for supplies.

canyon's

first tumble

...in the leaves

Canyon was six months old when his mom brought him up to Grandma's house to rake the leaves in their backyard. It was a cold brisk day and when Aimee put him in the leaves, he just sat there and didn't know what to think... then he grinned and decided he liked his bed of leaves.

October 1997

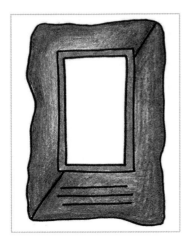

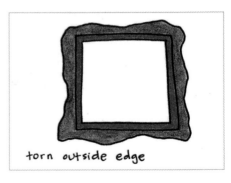

torn outside edge

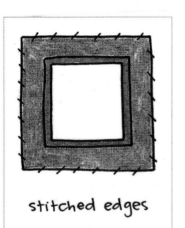

tilted mat

same colors, rearranged

stitched edges

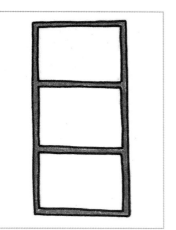

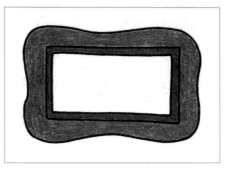

part of photo sticks out

photos in strips/
best for
scenic photos

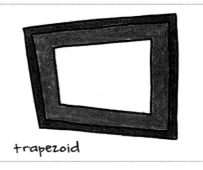

trapezoid

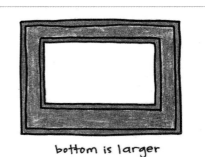

bottom is larger

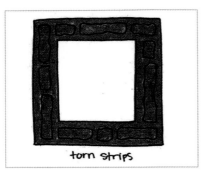

torn strips

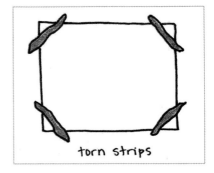

torn strips

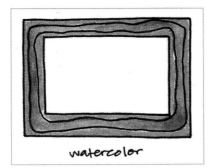

watercolor

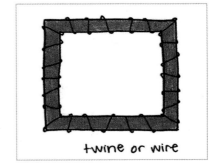

twine or wire

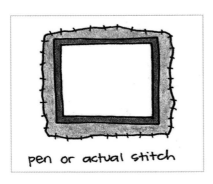

pen or actual stitch

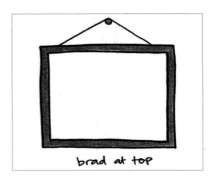

brad at top

mat is thick – thin – thick

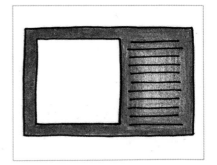

"burned" edges

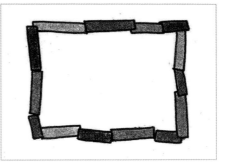

decorative edge

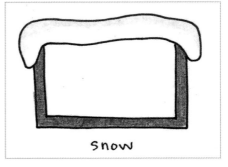

Snow

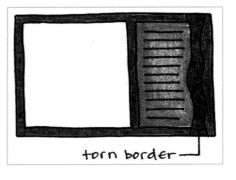

torn border

pattern paper

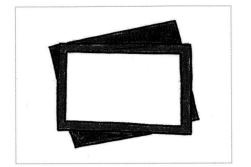

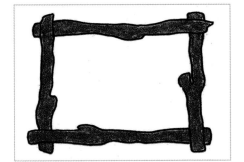

freeform edge

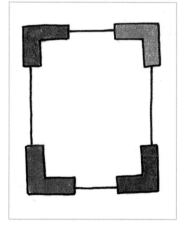

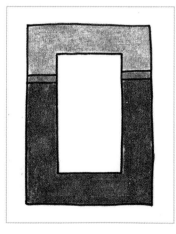

string

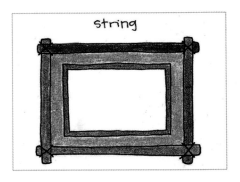

ribbon

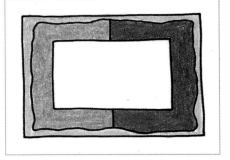

ribbon

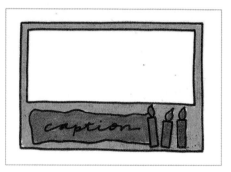

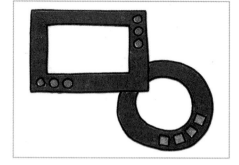

caption

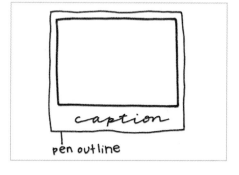

caption

pen outline

cardstock freeform outline

corners disconnected

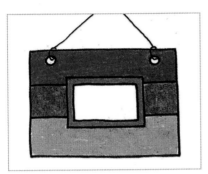

torn, stitched

torn strips

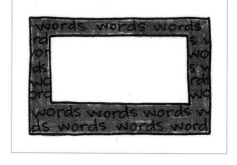

torn strips

knots
or
beads

for numbers
(such as a birthday)

vellum overlay

TITLE HERE

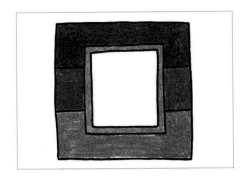

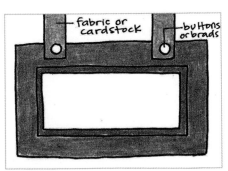

fabric or cardstock

buttons or brads

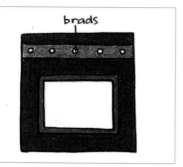

brads

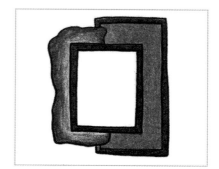

person's head sticks out

punched holes

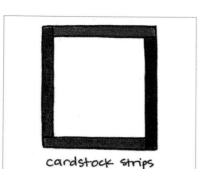

cardstock strips

2 photos

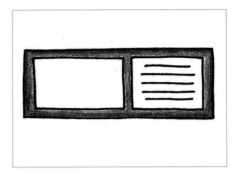

TITLE

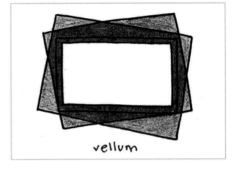

vellum

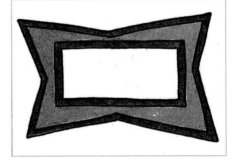

torn top

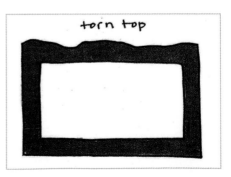

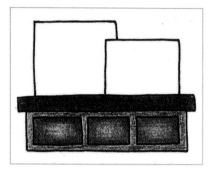

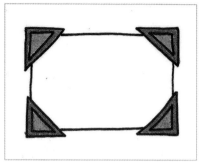

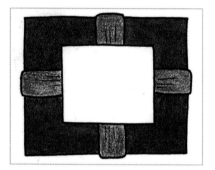

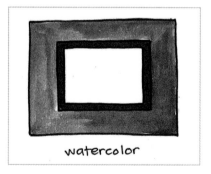

watercolor

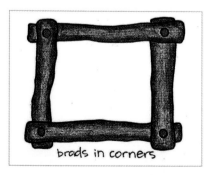

brads in corners

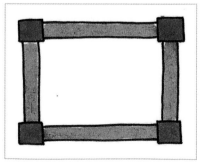

outer layer is torn

hand-drawn and chalked

TITLE

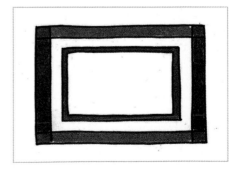

torn scraps

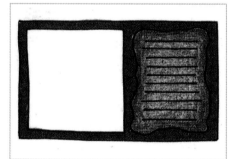

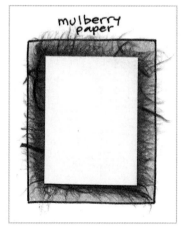

mulberry paper

freeform

photo on easel

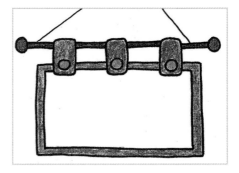

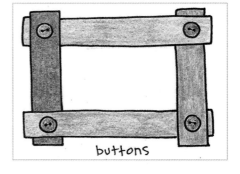

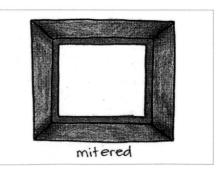

buttons

ribbon

mitered

photos connected with ribbon
or string, etc.

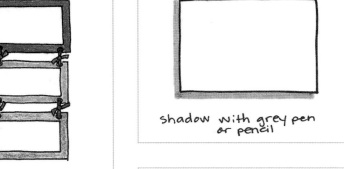

shadow with grey pen
or pencil

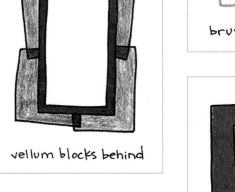

vellum blocks behind

brush pen as a border

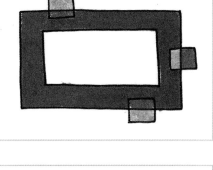

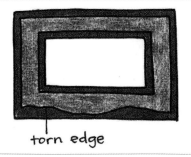

torn edge

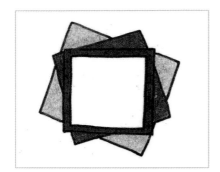

photographed frame
as mat

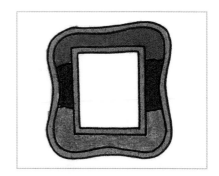

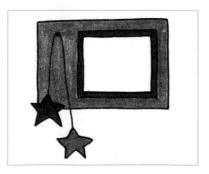

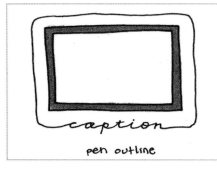

pen outline

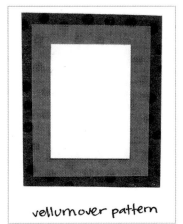

vellum over pattern

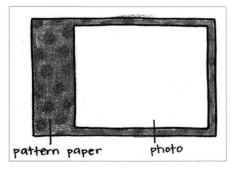

pattern paper   photo

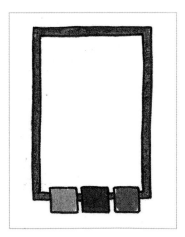

ribbon through slits
(cut with craft knife)

occasional button

double-torn edges

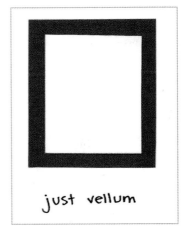

just vellum

actual stitches

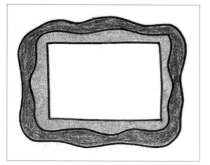

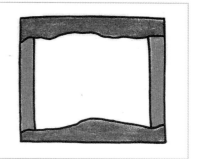

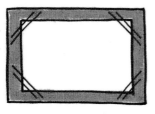

photo corners held down
with stitches

mulberry paper as
finishing touch

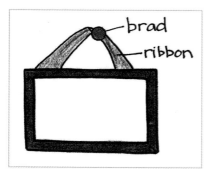

brad

ribbon

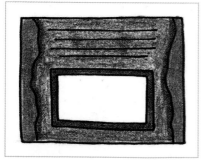

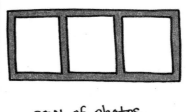

row of photos,
cut to same size

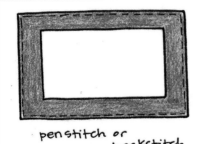

pen stitch or backstitch

journaling here!

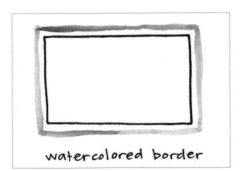

watercolored border

torn edges stitched

twine

some scraps cut, some torn

photo on clipboard

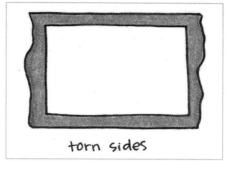

torn sides

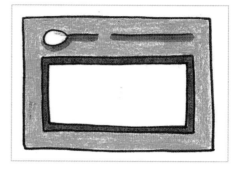

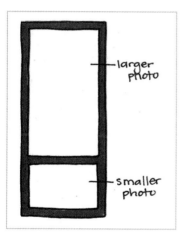

larger photo

smaller photo

thick mat with little stitches

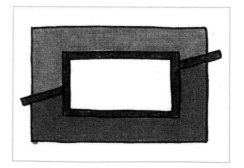

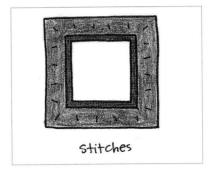

Stitches

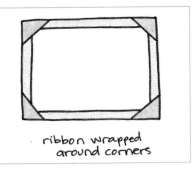

ribbon wrapped
around corners

torn
edge

torn
photo
edge
too!

ribbon

accents hang
from brads
and string

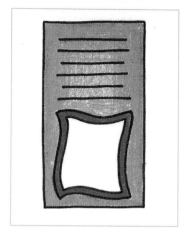

uneven
edges
around
circle

Word
word
WORD
WORD
word
word
word
WORD
word
word
WORD

"burned" edges

title

Hey

memorabilia
on mat

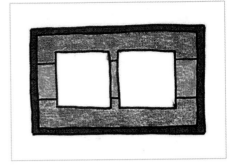

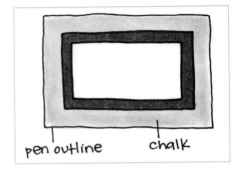

pen outline   chalk

String
around
edge
of mat

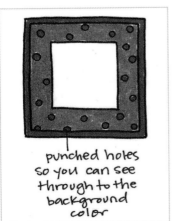

punched holes
so you can see
through to the
background
color

two torn halves, one crumpled

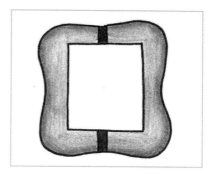

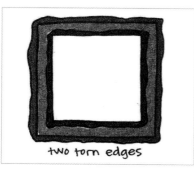

two torn edges

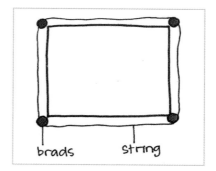

brads   string

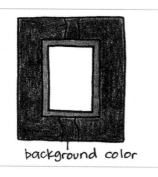

background color

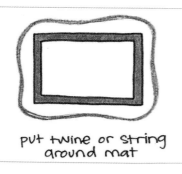

put twine or string
around mat

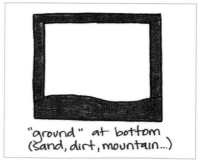

"ground" at bottom
(sand, dirt, mountain...)

buttons

button & string

ribbon through holes

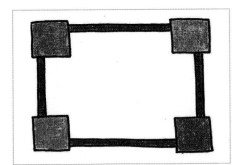

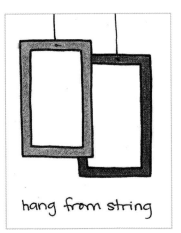

hang from string

PHOTO BY JOHN WAGNER

"Bliss"

SUPPLIES
Pressed flowers:
Nature's Pressed
Pen: Zig Millennium,
EK Success
Other: Ribbon
MCC inspiration: Becky
created the ribbon photo
corners using the sketch
on page 153.

"Our Easter Princess"

SUPPLIES
Pen: Zig Writer,
EK Success
Other: Ribbon
MCC inspiration:
Becky created the
photo mat using the
sketch on page 135.

PHOTOS BY MICHELE KENNEDY

"The Beach in Ft. Lauderdale"

SUPPLIES
Flip-flop stickers: Frances Meyer
Memorabilia holder: 3L
Pen: Pigma Micron, Sakura
Colored pencils: Prismacolor, Sanford
MCC inspiration: Becky created the photo mat using the sketch on page 153.

"Canyon's First Tumble"

SUPPLIES
Leaf punch: Emagination Crafts
Pen: Pigma Micron, Sakura
Colored pencils: Prismacolor, Sanford
MCC inspiration: Becky created the photo mat using the sketch on page 134.

PHOTOS BY JACQUE JENSEN

PHOTOS BY DANIEL HIGGINS

"Mountain Biking"

SUPPLIES
Patterned paper: Paperfever
Pen: Zig Writer, EK Success
MCC inspiration: Becky created the photo mat using the sketch on page 155.

"Hiking Timp"

SUPPLIES
Lettering template: The C-Thru Ruler Co.
Chalks: Stampin' Up!
Pen: Zig Writer, EK Success
MCC inspiration: Becky created the photo presentation using the sketch on page 130.

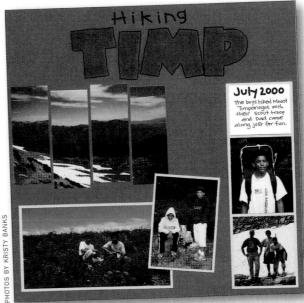

PHOTOS BY KRISTY BANKS

Odds & Ends

$\mathcal{U}$se these sketches when you're looking for something new to try on your pages. Here you'll find great ideas for backgrounds, pocket pages and interactive pages.

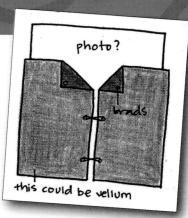

photo?

brads

this could be vellum

See page 191 for supplies.

Awards eArned in Middle School

skeletonized
leaves
all over
page

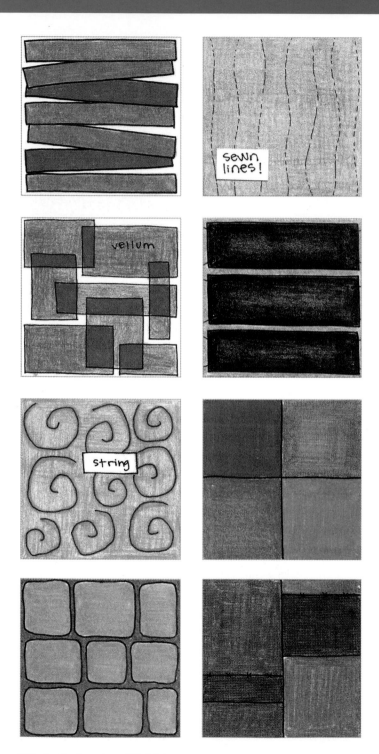

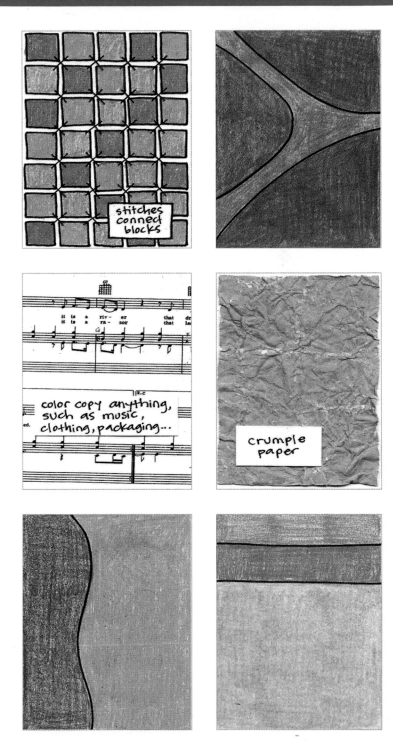

stitches connect blocks

color copy anything, such as music, clothing, packaging...

crumple paper

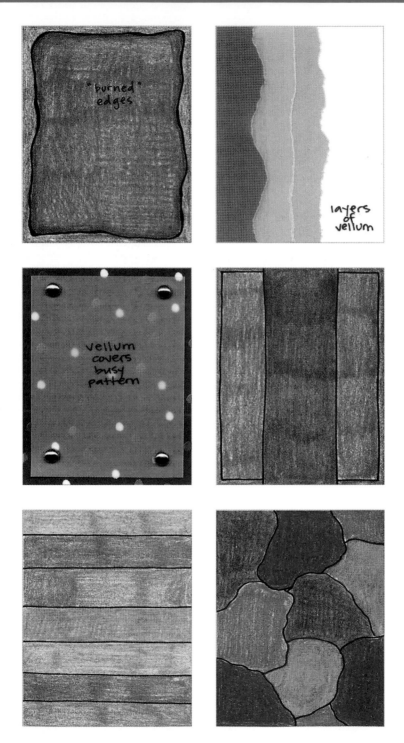

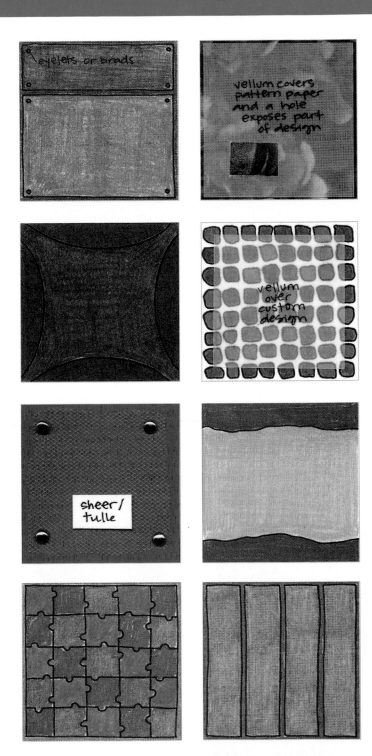

eyelets or brads

vellum covers
pattern paper
and a hole
exposes part
of design

vellum
over
custom
design

sheer/
tulle

woven strips

just strips
straight too?

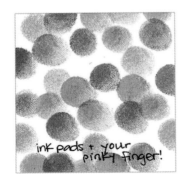

ink pads + your
pinky finger!

thick pattern strip

scraps of
mulberry

any
stamped
design

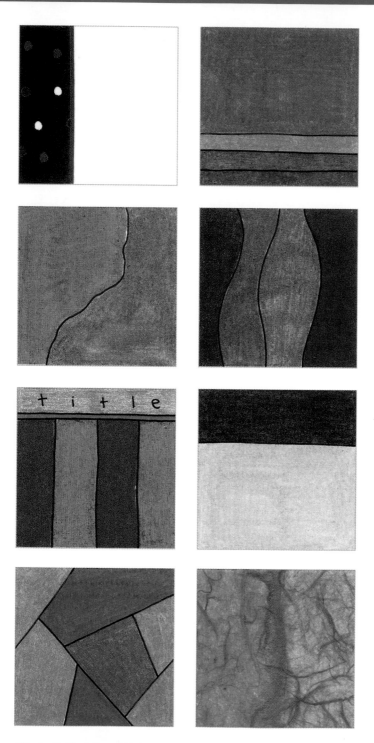

vellum
over
scraps

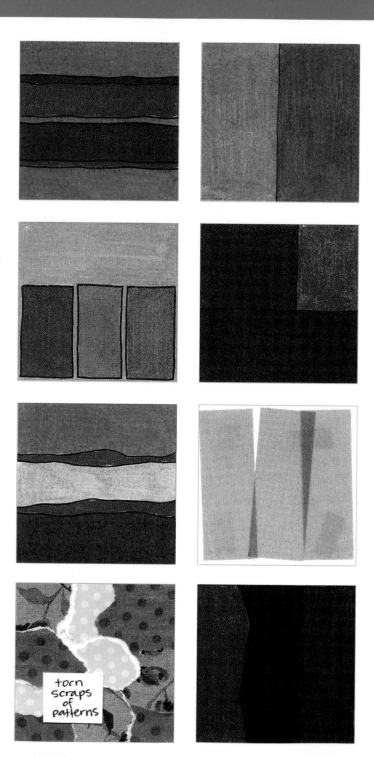

torn
scraps
of
patterns

sign accent is pocket

two pockets, connected

photo is pocket

crooked stitches

brads on top edge

all four sides of pocket are torn

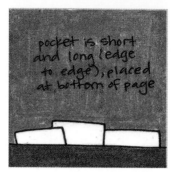

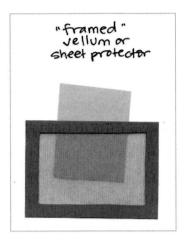

"framed"
vellum or
sheet protector

add decorative
edge at top
of pocket

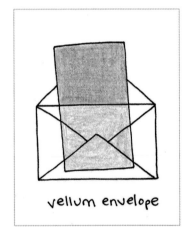

vellum envelope

brads are
especially
great for holding
pockets made
of vellum or
sheet protector

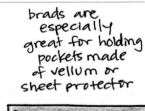

— brads

accents (such as punches) line top edge

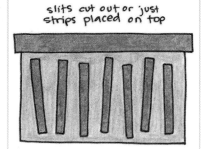

slits cut out or just strips placed on top

entire pocket lifted with mounting tape (or pop dots) for more room

Letters on top

edge to edge of the page, top of pocket

sheet protector

WORD

photo

stitched

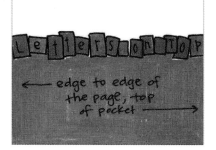

strips stitched together

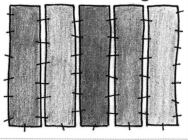

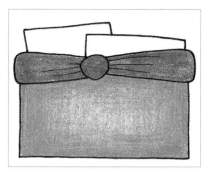

use instant frame (manufactured) for a pocket ... with vellum

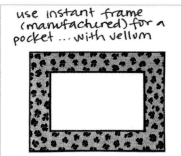

double
torn
layers

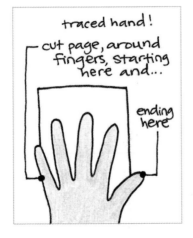

traced hand!

cut page, around
fingers, starting
here and...

ending
here

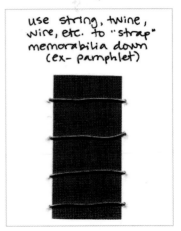

use string, twine,
wire, etc. to "strap"
memorabilia down
(ex- pamphlet)

simple pocket
made of sheet
protector (option:
print text on
the pocket)

BIRTHDAY
CARDS

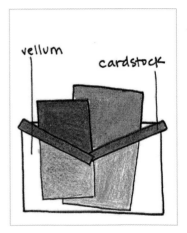

vellum

cardstock

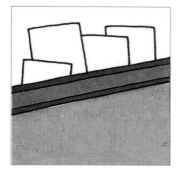

string
through
eyelets

layers of
pockets on
the side of
a layout

solid
or
mesh
bag

background

multiple pockets
on a page,
side by side

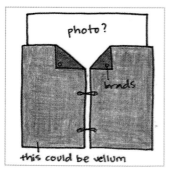

photo?

brads

this could be vellum

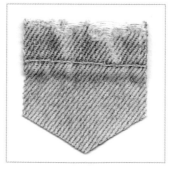

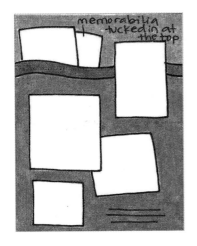

memorabilia
tucked in at
the top

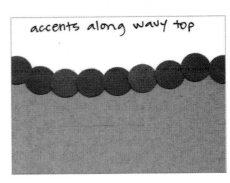

accents along wavy top

scenery
(ex-mountain)

ground

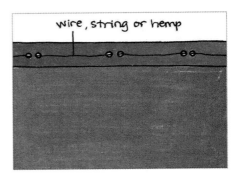

wire, string or hemp

just fabric

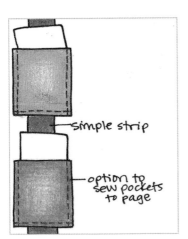

simple strip

option to
sew pockets
to page

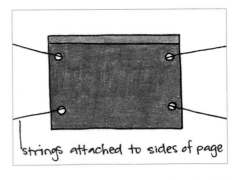

strings attached to sides of page

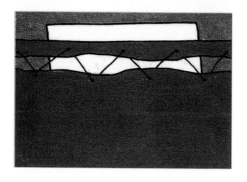

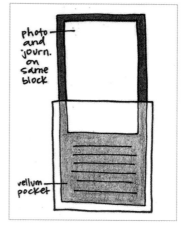

photo and journ. on same block

vellum pocket

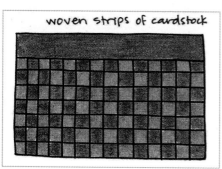

woven strips of cardstock

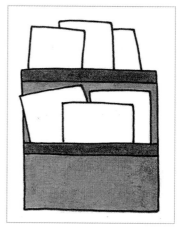

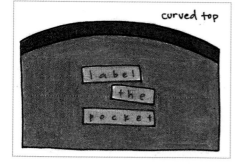

curved top

label the pocket

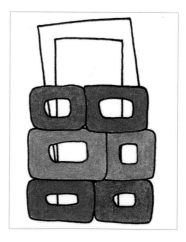

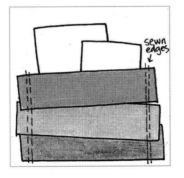

sewn edges

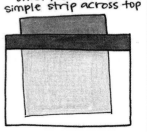

pocket made of vellum or sheet protector with simple strip across top

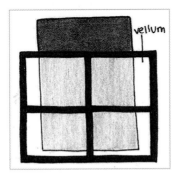

vellum

mini envelope

torn corner

eyelets with string

sheer fabric

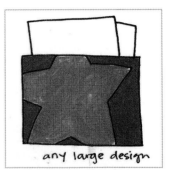

any large design

any hat design

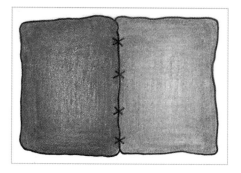

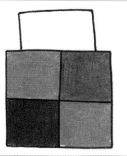

quarters can be solid or pattern papers

string wrapped around

pocket has hole

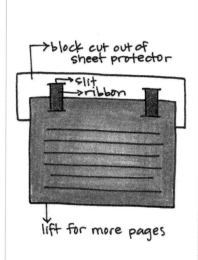

→ block cut out of
    sheet protector

→ slit
→ ribbon

lift for more pages

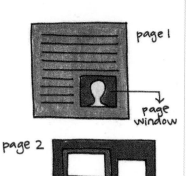

page 1

page window

page 2

Create a page window
by cutting a block out
of page 1 so that you
can see through to a
photo on page 2.

cut slit in sheet protector
at the top of pocket

long pockets like this
are great for holding
extra photos to save
space on layout

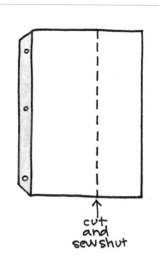

cut
and
sew shut

create a half page

PULL UP

before   after

Place your journaling block in a pocket so it can easily be pulled out. Journaling would be written on a tag with string at the top.

flaps closed

photo

flaps open

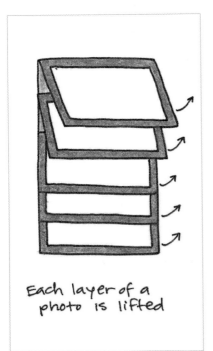

Each layer of a photo is lifted

this block is cut away from sheet protector

open flap and include several pages of photos or journaling (story book-like)

option: tie shut with a ribbon

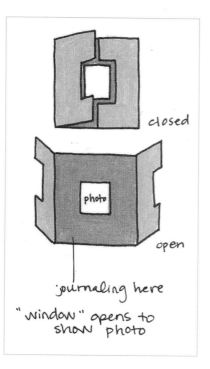

closed

photo

open

journaling here

"window" opens to show photo

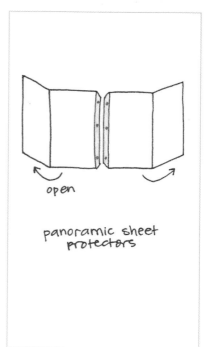

open

panoramic sheet protectors

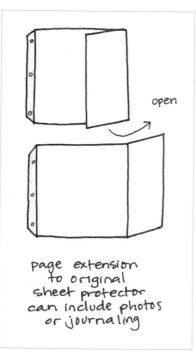

open

page extension to original sheet protector can include photos or journaling

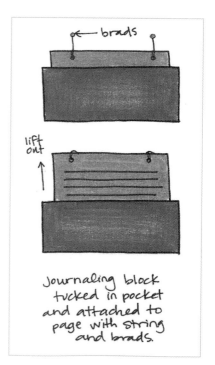

brads

lift out

Journaling block tucked in pocket and attached to page with string and brads.

lift

lift photo "flap"
to read journaling

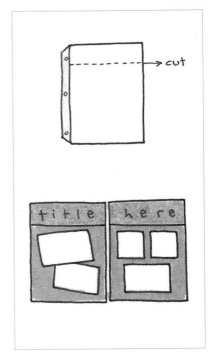

cut

title here

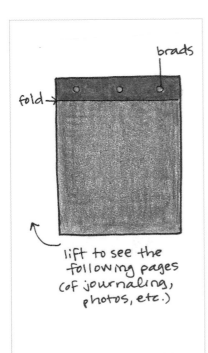

brads

fold →

lift to see the
following pages
(of journaling,
photos, etc.)

vellum over entire
page with
journaling...
covers "real" page

photo flip chart,
spiral-bound

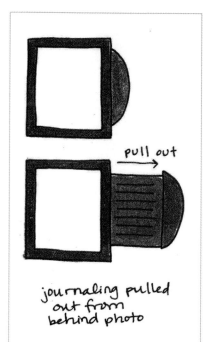

pull out

journaling pulled
out from
behind photo

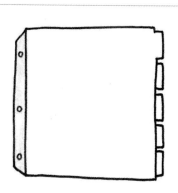

tabbed sections
in scrapbook,
defining events
or themes

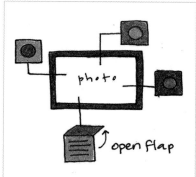

open flap

point out parts
of a photo and
include bits of
information,
history, facts, etc.
on "cards" where
you have to lift
little flaps

pages of photos
or journaling are
connected with
an eyelet

a memory button
records sound
for audio
memories!

Record a child's
voice, a clip of your
favorite music...

photo

open top & bottom
flaps to see photo

attach half-
sheet protectors
on the front of
one so the flaps
open up like a
door to full page

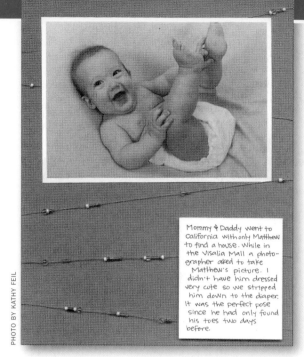

"Baby"

SUPPLIES
Pen: Zig Writer,
EK Success
Craft wire: Artistic Wire
Beads: Westrim
MCC inspiration: Becky
created the beaded
background using the
sketch on page 168.

Mommy & Daddy went to
California with only Matthew
to find a house. While in
the Visalia Mall a photo-
grapher asked to take
Matthew's picture. I
didn't have him dressed
very cute so we stripped
him down to the diaper.
It was the perfect pose
since he had only found
his toes two days
before.

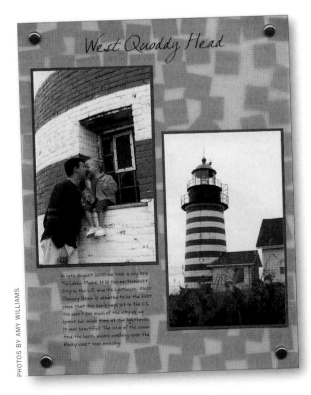

West Quoddy Head

"West Quoddy Head"

SUPPLIES
Vellum:
Paper Adventures
Computer fonts:
CK Bella, "The Best of
Creative Lettering" CD
Vol. 3 and CK Jot, "The
Art of Creative Lettering"
CD, *Creating Keepsakes*
Brads: American Pin
and Fastener
MCC inspiration: Becky
created the mosaic
background using the
sketch on page 171.

PHOTO BY VIVIAN SMITH

"Delos"

SUPPLIES
Vellum: Hot Off the Press
Computer font:
CK Sketch, "The Art of
Creative Lettering" CD,
Creating Keepsakes
Pen: Pigma Micron, Sakura
MCC inspiration: Becky
created the border pockets
using the sketch on
page 178.

"Awards"

SUPPLIES
Two-tone cardstock:
Paper Adventures
Brads: American
Pin and Fastener
Pen: Zig Writer,
EK Success
MCC inspiration:
Becky created the
sewn pocket using
the sketch on
page 178.

"The Story of Your Birth"

SUPPLIES
Patterned paper: Making Memories
Moon accent: My Mind's Eye
Pen: Zig Millennium,
EK Success
MCC inspiration: Becky
created the interactive
book using the sketch
on page 185.

PHOTOS BY ELINN ALLGAIER

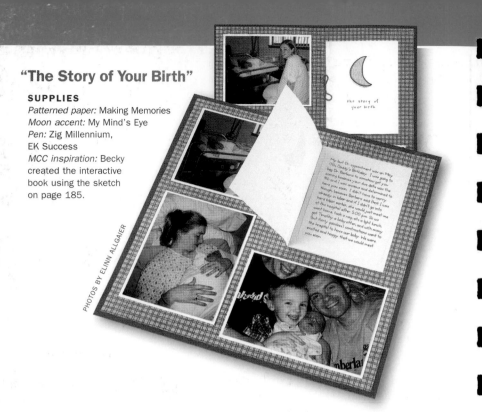

"All Decked Out"

SUPPLIES
Vellum: Paper Adventures
Computer font: CK Fun, "The
Art of Creative Lettering" CD,
Creating Keepsakes
Pen: Zig Writer, EK Success
MCC inspiration: Becky created
the vellum overlay using the
sketch on page 187.

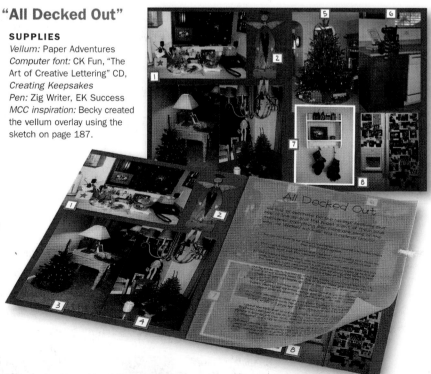